C000140449

ILLU

REALITY

Mary Taylor

BookLeaf
Publishing

ILLUSION OF REALITY © 2022 Mary Taylor

Presentation by *BookLeaf Publishing*

Web: www.bookleafpub.com

E-mail: info@bookleafpub.com

ISBN: 9789395756587

First edition 2022

DEDICATION

To my husband, Mike Taylor, my daughter,
Christina Nielsen, and my sons Terence Nielsen
and Jordan Taylor.

ACKNOWLEDGEMENT

The first people I would like to show my gratitude would be my parents, Merwin L and Doris E Nielsen. I wouldn't be here without you. You taught me so much and supported me in following my dreams and continue to do so from heaven. I couldn't have asked for better. I love you both so much.

Next would be Mike Taylor. my love, my twinflame, my everything. You give me the courage and strength to become a better person. I want to spend forever with you.

Then comes my sons. Terence Nielsen and Jordan Taylor. Terence, my son, you were my angel here on earth and are now my heavenly angel. I know that you are helping me every step of the way. I love and miss you so much.

Jordan, my son, you have always been so supportive and loving to me and all those around you. I am excited to see where the future takes you. I love and appreciate you so much.

Neisha Barry, My dear Aussy friend. Thank you for your guidance along my spiritual journey and for leading me to this opportunity.

Lisa Craig, my beautiful friend. You supported me when I decided to write again. Life is not the same without you although I get the clear signs you send me.

And to the Source of all things, my spirit guides, Natalie James, Lisa Allison and my TwinFlames soul family for their love and support along the way.

I AM

I am unique-there's no other quite like me

I am connected-with spirit and spirit with me

I am an Empath-I feel what you are feeling

I am a healer-for when your body needs healing

I am a reader-of oracle cards to help guide

I am a leader-to help others through life's wild ride

I am an artist-I love to create beautiful things

I am grateful-for what the universe brings

I am a mother-to other's children and to my own

I am a gardener-to the seeds that I have sown

I am a wife-to my husband and will always be

I am a lover-of positive things around me

I am a grieving mother-my son was taken way
too soon

I am energy-affected by the phases of the moon

I am a daughter-to parents that were the best

I am a baby sister-to siblings, way better than the
rest

I am a woman-I live life the best I can

Who am I, you ask? well..I AM.

WHAT IS NORMAL?

You say that I'm not normal
You say that I am a little bit odd
I know that I have weaknesses
I know that I am flawed

You say that I am crazy
You say that I am quite insane
But how can you really claim to know
What is going on inside my brain?

My views are not the same as
what you seem to believe
I just see things differently
Than the way that you perceive

So, who are you to tell me
That I am insane or not
When you know nothing of
the demons that I have fought

Am I a deranged lunatic?
Or perhaps a psychopath?
Am I a madman who spews
Their hatred, rage and wrath?

Perhaps I'm the one that's normal
And everyone else has gone insane
In which case, it will be
From sanity that I will abstain

I NEVER KNEW

I never knew that I was a poet who could create
a masterpiece with my words

By pouring out my soul onto paper talking about
my life's triumphs and my hurts

Sharing my emotions with all who are pulled to
read the words that I have written

Perhaps will bring out all of the emotions within
them that lay dormant and hidden

I never knew that the lyrics and melodies that
come from my mouth could heal

It's a dream that my son had before his death
that I have now been making real

The words, along with the tunes that seem to
flow through me from the Divine

Of my experiences giving hope to those who
have experiences same as mine

I never knew that by placing my paint covered
brush to canvas all that I could create

That with each brush stroke could be filled with
unconditional love or anger and hate

And that those who gaze upon them will feel the
emotion I felt in that precise second

Each tone and hue mixing and blending
beautifully together to your soul it beckons

I never knew that by weaving together mother
nature's vines can reach into dreams

An endless intricate web created by the sinews,
elaborately spun without any seams

Allowing your nightmares to be caught and
contained within this handcrafted latticework

Celestial connections being made through your
divine collaboration with Mother Earth

I never knew that with my skills and talents, that
I used to think were quite small

That through my artistic creativity that I could
affect other people's lives at all

But what I have begun to realize is that by
sharing this emotionally creative part of me

That within the deepest darkness, I can give
hope and light to help other people see

I'll never truly know how many people's lives
that I have impacted and touched

I will continue to strive to do so, though I don't
know if it will be enough

To help create a world that is better for all who
inhabit our Mother Earth

where we all stand strong in our light and know
our own true power and worth

FIRE WIFE

The life of a fire wife is an interesting one indeed.

I'm proud to stand by a man who helps those in need.

On call 24/7, fire radio's always on

Morning, noon and night some calls come before dawn.

For each call that he goes on, as he walks out of that door

An "I love you" and a quick kiss, unsure if I'll ever get more.

Each call that comes through is somebody's very bad day

Each call that he goes on "Bring them home safely" I pray

At home alone I wait, listening to the fire radio

"Firefighter down" are the words that I fear so

I ask myself "is it him?" is it the love of my life?

Will he make it home to his son and to me, his wife?

The life a fire wife can be a lonely one

Making plans together and for a lot of them he's gone

Off to fight fires on yet another day

Knowing I need to let him go, but really wanting him to stay.

Sometimes supporting the kids all alone

Mending and tending the seeds that you have sown

Not every woman can live in this life.

It takes a special woman to be a fire wife.

STRENGTH AGAINST
THE STORM

I can feel it coming, you know.

I can feel the atmospheric pressure plummet

As the thunderstorm approaches.

Although the pressure is falling,

it feels more like I'm being slowly crushed.

Every inch of my body begins to swell.

Slowly taking on this uninvited guest,

this inflammation of unknown origin.

My fingers, toes and joints are stiff

and becoming more so

with each passing moment

As the day progresses and

as the storm draws near,

the power of the energy grows

It becomes harder to sit still,

I unsuccessfully try to focus

on anything just to take my

attention away from the ever

intensifying pain.

The aggravation and irritation

have made themselves known.

Mole hills become mountains,

the calming effects of a babbling brook

gradually turning into the madness

and chaos of whitewater.

Here I am atop this inadequate canoe,

being carried along by the current

without any way of controlling the direction

or the speed of which I am being propelled.

The inflammation continues

throughout my body,

my rib cage is screaming

as the bones begin to break

Outside the storm is raging,

lightning crashes, thunder booms

The trees are being violently thrashed about

by the pure strength of the winds.

The tears are flowing by this point,

I wonder why I have this burden to carry,

It feels like I've been cursed.

I am rocking back and forth,

trying to comfort myself

as you would a fussy baby.

The pressure continues to increase,

my body feels like it can't

possibly take any more.

Then, as with all storms

this one begins to ease.

The winds die down

The thunder and lightning conclude

their overture for the evening.

The pressure changes,

 the air feels lighter.

Although many times the pain remains.

It'll hold on for days, or sometimes weeks

And it truly wears away at your resolve.

This intense pain is hard to deal with

But it's has shown me my strength,

it has shown me that I am truly blessed

to have the ability to get through these times.

Some have witnessed this tremendous fight

It can be rather scary,

I'd say to see someone in so much misery,

The helplessness that must be felt by all.

I have been through these many times

in the 25 years since it started.

This wasn't the first and unfortunately,

I know this won't be the last.

From now until the next,

I'll enjoy each day as I can,

and I'll continue to make my way through,

to show my strength against the storm

until my dying day.

TO SEE YOU AGAIN

As I hold my sweet baby girl

I am in such awe of your beauty

Your tiny hands and tiny feet

You are as perfect as can be

Your olive skin, and raven hair

A true angel here on earth

I feel so blessed that I could be

the vessel of your birth

I hold you in my arms and press

You tight against my broken heart

The pain I feel right now is all

To give you a worthy start

I knew right away that mine,

you were not meant to be

I was meant to bring you here

And provide you another family

To love you and to support you

The way that I wished I could do

But everything I sacrificed

Was all for my love of you

The last day that I held you

Was 31 long years ago

Over the years my love has grown

And oh, how I miss you so.

One day soon, I hope,

I can hold you in my warm embrace

To look into your eyes once more

And place a kiss upon your face.

I can't wait to hear of how

The years of your life have gone

I just hope that I don't have to wait

To see you, very long.

MY BABY BOY

I feel you move inside of me   as you grow

What the future brings, I just don't know

But I am so filled with such hope and love

In receiving this precious gift from source above

Looking down at your tiny sweet face

see within your divine power and grace

That I hope stays with you throughout your life

Through the good times and thru times of strife

Sending you off to kindergartens first day

hard letting go so you can find your own way

Then in the blink of an eye you became a man

Knowing your next step and following the plan

Even from a small child you've been so smart

And love so deeply from the bottom of your heart

You've always been there to support your friends

A good head on your shoulders and common sense

I'm so proud of the man that stands before me now

The time flew by so quickly and I don't know how

Blessed for the time you've spent growing into who you are now

And for the years on this earth that we're allowed

You have Within you a very wise and old soul

I see in you with each tried and every achieved
goal

baby boy, I'm amazed at the man you've
become

And I know what ever life brings that you will
overcome

Oh, my baby boy, oh baby boy, oh my boy

my baby boy, I'm so proud that you' are my son

being your mother is a lottery that I've won

You've Become the man that I'd always
dreamed you be

blessed that when you picked a mom that you
chose me

A MOTHERS LOVE

A mother's love is ignited long before your birth

And moms seem to know right away how much
your life is worth

We feel you grow inside of us growing more
with each new day

one day you'll be amazing and nothing will stand
in your way

Oh, Mama can you hear me our connection has
just begun

I'm coming down from heaven above I'm
coming to be your son

Mama, I can hear you I'm excited to start my life

to grow up big and strong like dad and one day
meet my wife

you teach us moms so much even as we are
teaching you

all those things you'll need to know what you'll
need your whole life through

respect good values and numbers and words like
I love you

and all of the beautiful colors like the red, the
white and the blue

your body it grew stronger and your mind and
soul did too

and as the years went rushing by a fine man you
grew into

You taught me so much Mama what you taught
me as I grew you

you see I listened and learned a lot as a man it
helped me through

you fed and clothed me Mama and with
everything we went through

you and dad were there to support me please tell
dad I love him too

and to my little brother I love you and I'll miss
you so

I'll watch your life from heaven above and I'm
so proud of you, bro

a mother's love is something that can never be
undone

no matter which mistakes are made he'll forever
be her son

She'd give up everything for him she'd give up
her own life

to make his life a bit easier to ease a bit of a
strife

a mother's love is something that nothing else
can quite compare

a mother's love that's for her child there's
nothing stronger is there

dad he taught me manners, you showed me how
to hope again

you taught me to believe in myself and
comforted me when I was in pain

and in my opinion Mama, I couldn't have asked
for more

I feel how much you love me Mama even death
it has endured

my love for you it started long before your first
breath

each day has made it stronger even after your
death

a mother's love has made me stronger than I
thought I'd be

and when I feel your spirit close, I feel the love
you have for me

Mama I'm so sorry I hurt you and for all of the
mistakes I made

for betraying the trust that we had and for not
choosing the right way

my journey here upon this earth was shorter than
I thought it'd be

it soon became my time to go it was all part of
God's plan you see

a mother's love is something that can never be
undone

no matter which mistakes are made he will
forever be her son

she'd give up everything for him she'd give up
her own life

to make his life a bit easier to ease a bit of his
strife

a mother's love is something that nothing else
can quite compare

a mother's love that's for her child there's
nothing stronger is there

cry the tears you need to Mama for I'll be right
there with you

I'll wrap my wings around you Mama and I'll
send you my love too

oh, Mama can you hear me my death can't be
undone

I'll wait for you and heaven above I'll see you
soon your loving son

ONE LAST EMBRACE

Awakened from a deep slumber by the shrill
phones ring

My heart drops in fear of what this phone call
may bring

I Answer with shallow hello, and confirm my
identity

And then I heard the words that will forever stay
with me

He said my son's name with a sad melancholy
tone

my son had been killed and not much else is
known

I woke from a dream and stepped into a
nightmare

Sobbing I screamed out "not my son, It's not fair"

To God in heaven, I pled and I earnestly prayed

Begging for Him not to take my son away

My broken heart pounds as I walk through the door

It has been shattered, thousands of pieces lie on the floor

I don't know how I will make it through this awful day

Identifying my son's body, there has to be some mistake

I see his body lying there covered in a sheet of white

If I can just wake from this nightmare, I know he'd be alright

No matter how I tried, this horrible dream becomes real

I Fall to my knees sobbing, it all seems so surreal

Lying before me is my oldest son, and now his life is gone

my world has stopped, I don't know how I will continue on

someone else took my sons life force and stopped its flow

How could this have happened? I'm not sure I'll ever know

I look down at his lifeless body, and I touch his cold hand

Pleading with God to make it not so, to help me understand

Such a beautiful spirit taken too early from this
earth

He impacted so many people, starting on the day
his birth

As I stand here beside him, as his life flashes
before my eyes

It's so unfair that to my son I have to say my
goodbyes

As the drops of heartbreak stream down my
tear-stained face

I kiss your face one last time, giving you one last
embrace

MY GUIDE

I can see her features slowly begin to appear as she

manifests herself before me

The first time she showed herself to me

I was quite frightened, as I'm sure you can imagine

She told me her name is L'Orion and that

She is an elder from another timeline sent here

To help aid and guide me on my life's path

"Crossing between the dimensions, isn't as

difficult as it may seem" she told me once

"All it takes is to truly believe"

When she is in the earthly realm, she is a beautiful

Young woman but in other realms she looks very different

I caught a glimpse of her once as she came through to me

Her hair and skin looked like the roots from a tree

Rough, hard, cracked and colorless

I was amazed at the stark difference between the way she looked when she appeared to me here and her "true" appearance

When I saw her, there were so many questions that

raced through my mind, but the one that fell from my lips was

"Are you an elemental?"

She told me she was that and so much more

That my human mind could not even comprehend

"You are meant to be a great being upon this earth who teaches and inspire many" she told me

"Future generations will speak of you the way that you speak of your ancestors"

My ancestors consist of witches, prophets and shaman, so many great and powerful people

Whose actions and deeds made their lives worthy of talking about

I reacted with shock and dismay

"Who? Me?" I asked

She laughed and gently nodded

I couldn't believe what she was telling me

How could this be true?

My mind began to race, and memories began to flood my consciousness

Time after time, experience after experience I was shown all the things I had done

Throughout my lifetime and I had never realized the truth behind it all

I stood there slack jawed and speechless

I had no idea the extent of the power that flows within me

The unlimited potential that had been laid at my feet and I had not even known it was there

I felt overwhelming awe, and a little bit of guilt because of the time not knowing

Once again, she laughed gently and with a smile said to me softly

"It was all part of the divine plan"

She explained that to me that this earth is a place of learning, experience and remembering all that we have always conceptually known

She told me "The time has now come for you to step into the power that you have been given."

That is why she came in the first place

Since then, she has become my teacher, my
guide and my friend

As I sit here writing this my thoughts keep going
to something that has stuck in my head since the
day, she spoke it

"You are in control of your own existence on
this earth. All of your dreams will come true if
you truly believe it to be,"

Such a simple statement yet it was so profound

That day, with those few words that she spoke
had changed everything.

Changed the way that I look at life

I vowed that day that I would step into the
power that I have been given and that I would
use this gift for the greatest good

So…

One step at a time….

One day at a time…

I will learn what I need to do to become who I am meant to be and in doing so I just may be able to make this world a better place for all.

A SPIRIT GUIDES MESSAGE

As I sit here looking deep into your eyes

I can see the pain and sorrow burning within you

The pieces of your heart broken from all the lies

The anger and hate you've allowed to stew

I see the darkness that surrounds your soul

As it tries to snuff out your divine light

Making your soul dark is their evil goal

Your flame though small still shines bright

Can you feel me here sitting beside you?

Holding your soft hand lovingly in mine?

Can you feel this celestial love, so pure and true?

It's golden warmth, an embrace from the divine

Don't you know that I'm with you, every step of the way

Through whatever challenges this life brings?

I'm with you through all the nights and days

Through all of this life's ends and beginnings

Due to free will, you have to ask for my aid

Just tell me what makes you worry and fear

I've been Here Through each decision you've made

Through all of the happiness, failures and tears

I send you messages, symbols and signs each
day

So many attempts I've made to get your attention

I can help aide you in keeping the darkness at
bay

The more we communicate, the stronger our
connection

Close your eyes and you will be able to see me

I'll visit you in the quiet times and in your
dreams

Showing you the truth of what was and will be

And helping you understand what it all means

This bond goes beyond your space and time

Beyond what your earthly mind can understand

I come from realms of the ethereal, and divine

Far away galaxies beyond the stars are my
homeland

Close your eyes and you will be able to see me

Ill visit you in the quiet times and in your
dreams

Showing you the truth of what was and will be

And helping you understand what it all means

I'll hold your hand through life as you make
your way

I'll be there beside you even through the darkest
night

Walking at your side is where I will always stay

Helping you stand strong within your own
divine light

THE OCEANS FLOW

"I think I know why the ocean flows" (Vijay Pandit)

A wise old woman once said to me

as we gazed out upon the moonlit sea together.

"Imagine if you were being pushed & pulled at the whim of Grandmother moon.

Imagine being twisted and turned as if you were bread dough

being kneaded by Mother Nature Herself and all the while being ever

powerful in your own right."

She explained how the ocean, in a single drop can be brushed away like a teardrop upon the cheek of the earth by the fingertip of mankind; but in an accumulated amount it has the ability to move mountains, and to create vast valleys

It allows us to travel upon it, enjoy its beautiful beaches all over the world, and then feeds us with its abundance. It has the power to wipe out cities with tsunamis and floods; or can aid in the growth of plant life that is vital to our very survival.

The Ocean is so powerful that it can coerce even the most destructive volcanic lava into cooling, creating beautiful islands, and holding within it a whole other world teeming with life, so vast that much of it is still yet to be discovered.

It possesses all of this power but is it truly free?

I wonder, does each drop feel lonely and weak on its hydro-logical journey, and then as it falls from the sky?

Or is it content in the knowledge of its forthcoming oceanic reunion? That inevitable merging together of each tiny drop that ultimately transforms it back into the ever-powerful ocean.

Day after day, Grandmother Moon moves consistently through her phases. Growing, new to full then shrinking back to anew. Waxing and waning, constantly rotating and orbiting in perfect rhythm with the ebb and flow of the tides. Dancing together, flawlessly, as they have since the beginning of time in precise synchronization.

Some out there may call me crazy,

I'm sure I'm little bit odd, at the very least.

But as I gaze upon the ocean's waves, I can almost feel the pull.

That wise old woman made me see things differently and it helped me understand So much throughout my lifetime.

So today,

I'm passing this wisdom on to you,

as that wise old woman once did for me.

"I think I know why the ocean flows......"

Inspired by the words of poetrysoup poet Vijay Pandit "I think I know why the ocean flows"-From her poem: I think I know why the ocean flows.

LAND OF NOD

As I lay here, a midst the witching hour

Listening to the muted beat of the raindrops as
they land

Upon the tin roof above my head

My mind is cluttered with thought about

What happened that day and what may happen
in the next

Mingled with random memories from points of
childhood long forgotten

After admitting defeat to my thought processes

I sit up and watch the raindrops appear

And then make their journey down the
windowpane and into

The puddle created by its friends and family
below

I am mesmerized by the neon lights flashing

Creating a metronome of light within the
darkness

From my window, the rain blurs the neon light

Making them look distorted and out of sorts

Flashing on and off to the beat of the raindrops
overhead

I watch the shadows as they grow and retreat

With the light from the neon-signs,

Momentarily hypnotizing me

The streets are quiet, not a person or vehicle in
sight

So, I lie back down and close my eyes

Still seeing the glow of the neon lights through my eyelids

I listen to the beat of the raindrops above

My thoughts begin to slow

The flashing light begins to fade

And I finally begin to fall

Ever so slowly....

Into

The Land of Nod

WRITERS BLOCK

I stare blankly at the cursor on the screen

Watching it as it blinks off and on

Searching for one small thought or idea

A spark that can be built upon

In the hands of an author or poet

Words are a powerful tool

In the right hands can make you rich

And the wrong will make you look like a fool

When the poets' words have stalled

Or when the thoughts and ideas have died

It becomes figuratively as if

The poets' hands are tied

Without words and ideas to build upon

A poet's page will remain blank and bare

So, until a thought appears in my mind

At this page I will blankly stare

FIRE CALL

Tones blare

Heart pounds

Prayers sent

Station bound

Turnouts on

Nomax too

Helmet, gloves

And rubber boots

18-09

That is me

Sirens sing

Engine gleams

Air pack on

Arrive on scene

Cars on fire

Patients scream

Hoses pulled

Scene assessed

Flames put out

Jaws of life spread

Patient care

EMS on scene

Life-flight inbound

Punctured spleen

Patient gone

Hospital bound

Head back home

Til next time around

LAPIS LAZULI DREAM

Intense blue light energy

Radiates from the

manifestation stone

bringing balance and

a voice to speak

your personal truth.

It provides wisdom and

connects us to the mystical

and spiritual realms.

The key to total

spiritual attainment.

Breathe... Let go...

Lapis Lazuli Dream

THE PRECIPICE OF THE UNKNOWN

As I stand here upon

the precipice of the unknown

I stare out into the darkness

Full of uncertainty and fear

Afraid of taking the next step

What if I fall?

What if I don't?

What would that mean?

I stand here on the

Brink of the abyss

Not knowing what to do,

But understanding that

the next step I take

Could change the

course of my life.

But yet I just stand here

Wondering....

Every possible "what if" scenario

flows through my mind

Each thought creating

more fear and doubt

Making it impossible for my brain

To control the movement of my feet.

Here I stand on the edge

of this phantasmic chasm

Looking out into the

darkness of the unknown

Trembling from the fear

that consumes me

Paralyzed by the terror

that envelopes me

I take a deep breath,

And then another

Which allows me

to take back command

of my body and mind

I close my eyes and then,

Ever so slowly…

my foot begins to move

As I take that first step

into the unknown.

VOLUNTEER FIREFIGHTERS

Sitting   enjoying dinner with his family one
summer night

Fire radio blares a sign of someone's plight

Dropping whatever he's doing and, he runs to a
stranger's aid

Quickly changing whatever plans that he had
made

hugs and kisses his wife and kids as he tells
them goodbye

There is a chance that on this call that he may
die

His heart pounds waiting for whatever may
come next

fire fully involved is what it said in the text

90 seconds turnouts on, packed up, in the fire engine they go

Lights flashing, sirens blaring to help quicken the flow

Battling the fire armed with only a fire hose

Toxic smoke makes it hard to see past their nose

Risking their lives for people that they don't even know

Many times, with no gratitude shown

Volunteer firefighters are who these heroes are

Men and women doing it from the kindness of their hearts

They don't do it for money, fame or to get recognized

They do it for their community, and for the betterment of our lives

Volunteering their time, at all times of the night or day

It's time for us to show them our gratitude, I'd say

Thank you for being a hero

Thank you volunteers

FOREVER WITH YOU

From the moment that we met

I knew that it was you

As soon as I looked into your eyes

I knew this love was true

From the first words you said to me

and the words that I replied

Since then, it's been on

each other that you and I have relied

love so strong, it can't be denied

Our hearts together are now forever tied

Finding and loving each other

through many lifetimes

Where I have been yours and

where you have been mine

we fit together like puzzle pieces so perfectly

Two halves of the same whole created together
don't you see

Made as one at the start of eternity

Coming together time and again you and me

I knew that it was you

There's nothing that I could do

But fall in love with you

Twin flame love

is a love that's true

Seems we always knew,

from Day 1 I knew I loved you,

Grateful that I said I do

I want to spend forever with you

GOLDEN FAIRY

As dusk slowly creeps in,

Just as the sun begins

To duck its head behind the trees,

causing the shadows to stretch

and distort into dark, haunting figures.

A golden sparkle catches my eye

It flutters and flitters about,

Growing larger and brighter

as it comes closer.

I blink my eyes several times.

I can't believe what it is

that I am seeing.

Before me is

the most beautiful fairy.

Her golden hair and wings

Sparkle in the fading sunlight.

Her gown is made of the finest silk,

finer than I have ever had

the pleasure of looking upon.

She has a warm, comforting glow

that surrounds her tiny body and

the warm feeling of unconditional love

that seems to radiate from her

Making you feel safe and secure

Like the feeling of a

loving mothers embrace

Or perhaps like being in

the arms of the

Christ Consciousness itself.

I wonder if I am dreaming

And as if in answer she spoke

"This is not a dream"

One would think that

such a small being would

have a voice to match

but as she spoke the

sound touched my heart and soul.

It filled me with hope.

I was in awe of this small being

that held such power within her.

She opened her mouth

once more to speak

All that came this time

was a shrill buzzing noise.

Surely this couldn't have come

from this beautiful creature.

Once again, the shrill, piercing noise.

I knew that noise, but from where?

I closed my eyes to try to remember.

When I opened them again,

I was back in my bed.

My room was the hue of the setting sun.

The disappointment filled me,

I glanced out the window

and saw a golden sparkle.

LIFE'S EXPERIENCE

This life is about the experience

of each thing that happens to you

Allowing you the opportunity

to show others the you that is true

It allows you to truly show up

the way you were meant to be

To experience life in the kind of way

that you are truly free

When you look at this life as a performance

one where you have the artistic right

To live life through your character

and to stand in your spiritual light

Looking at each experience in life

as an energetical exchange

It makes you view life differently,

and makes it not quite so strange

Life is a roller coaster,

this is something we all know

But it's all about the experiences

that allow our souls to grow

Each person that we meet or

that happens to cross our path

Whether that meeting was happy or

one that is filled with wrath

Each one gives us a choice on

how to respond or react

How we choose to respond

creates what we will attract

The next time you have an experience

remember that you have a choice

Are you going to respond with anger or

are you going be grateful and rejoice?

However, you choose to respond

reflects in your energy

Whatever it is that you believe

is exactly how life your will be.

Lightning Source UK Ltd.
Milton Keynes UK
UKHW020709030223
416413UK00013B/1973

9 789395 756587